SMALL APARTMENTS
PETITS APPARTEMENTS
KLEINE APPARTEMENTS

SMALL APARTMENTS
PETITS APPARTEMENTS
KLEINE APPARTEMENTS

evergreen

EVERGREEN is an imprint of

Taschen GmbH

© 2005 TASCHEN GmbH

Hohenzollernring 53, D-50672 Köln

www.taschen.com

Editor Editrice Redakteur:
Simone Schleifer

French translation Traduction française Französische Übersetzung:
Marion Westerhoff

German translation Traduction alemande Deutsche Übersetzung:
Grusche Rosenkranz

English proof reading Relecture anglaise Korrektur lesen:
Matthew Clarke

Art director Direction artistique Art Direktor:
Mireia Casanovas Soley

Graphic design and layout Mise en page et maquette Graphische Gestaltung und Layout:
Diego González

Printed by Imprimé en Gedruckt durch:
Anman Gràfiques del Vallès, Spain

ISBN: 3-8228-4178-1

In the second half of the 20th century, two main trends in modern living emerged, in response to the characteristics of our times. On the one hand, residences now act as interior landscapes and, along with other compact elements of contemporary life, they serve to save time, motion and money. These developments typify life in today's big cities and they have impinged on the design of small living spaces. On the other hand, the density of large cities and the desire for an individualized home is constantly increasing, bringing in their wake a new kind of space: the small apartment. The deterioration of habitable areas is reflected inside homes by a reduction of the surface area to minimal proportions.

The layout of small apartments is similar to regular-size dwellings, and even the tiniest of apartments can have some extra touches, such as studios or reading niches. The major difference lies in the strategies that architects and designers use to take full advantage of the space and emphasize the architectural features of each home. These apartments stand out precisely because of the ingenious way in which housing needs have been adapted to minimal space without sacrificing quality or comfort.

Many interior design strategies are common to all these apartments. We can find many examples in which the same space serves a number of different functions. Innovative strategies include walls that stop short of the ceiling or side walls; sliding doors that disappear; mobile screens that permit changes in an apartment's layout; or openings and translucent materials that allow light to flow through separated areas. Although they all find their own particular solutions, by combining design strategies that use space to full advantage, they share five aspects that are essential to successful interior design and the most important features of such an apartment: functional furnishings, color, movable panels, restraint, and the exterior.

This compilation of projects from around the world pays special attention to the particular features of each space, within the common restriction of a limited surface area. The range of projects will be of interest to not only architects and designers but also residents of modern cities, thereby creating a basic tool for understanding how architects, designers, or owners of small apartments approach a project involving minimal living space.

La deuxième moitié du XXe siècle voit l'émergence de deux tendances principales dans le mode de vie contemporain, nées des caractéristiques de notre époque. D'une part, les résidences se transforment en paysages intérieurs et répondent en même temps aux contraintes liées au gain de temps, de déplacement et d'argent inhérents à la vie contemporaine. Evolution qui définit la vie actuelle dans les grandes villes et conduit au design de petits espaces de vie. D'autre part, la densité des grandes villes et le désir de personnaliser le logement ne cessent de croître, donnant ainsi naissance à un nouvel espace : le petit appartement. La réduction des zones habitables et la diminution de l'espace de vie se traduisent donc par la tendance au minimalisme.

La conception de petits appartements est semblable à celle de logements de taille normale : même le plus petit des appartements peut avoir des petites touches originales comme un bureau ou un coin lecture. La différence essentielle réside dans la stratégie envisagée par les architectes ou les designers pour optimiser l'espace et exalter les concepts architecturaux de chaque habitation. Ces appartements se distinguent par l'ingéniosité déployée pour adapter les besoins domestiques à un espace minimal sans sacrifices de qualité ou de confort.

Bon nombre de ces stratégies de design intérieur sont communes à tous ces appartements. Les multiples exemples d'espaces polyvalents, accueillant diverses fonctions, en sont la preuve. Ces approches innovatrices développent de nombreux concepts : murs qui ne touchent ni le plafond ni les murs latéraux, portes coulissantes escamotables, cloisons mobiles permettant de moduler le plan de l'appartement ou encore ouvertures et matériaux translucides qui laissent passer la lumière dans les zones séparées. En combinant les concepts de design qui optimisent l'espace, chacune de ces stratégies propose une solution différente. Néanmoins, elles partagent toutes cinq éléments, essentiels à la réussite du design intérieur et typiques de ce genre d'appartement : mobilier fonctionnel, couleurs, cloisons et panneaux amovibles, restrictions et concept d'extérieur.

Cette collection de projets du monde entier met en relief les données particulières de chaque espace dont le dénominateur commun est la réduction de la surface habitable. Cet éventail de projets intéressera non seulement les architectes et les designers mais aussi les habitants des villes modernes. C'est un outil de base qui permet de comprendre l'approche développée par les architectes, les designers et les propriétaires de petits appartements pour réaliser un espace de vie minimaliste.

In der zweiten Hälfte des 20. Jh. kamen zwei neue Wohntrends auf, die im Zeichen der heutigen Zeit stehen. Einerseits sind unsere Häuser und Wohnungen zu einer inneren Landschaft geworden, andererseits dienen sie neben anderen, kompakten Elementen des modernen Lebens dazu, Zeit, Bewegung und Geld zu sparen. Diese Entwicklung prägt das Leben in den modernen Großstädten und wirkt sich auf die Gestaltung kleiner Wohnräume aus. Auch sind Großstädte dicht besiedelt und der Wunsch nach einem individuellen Wohnraum wächst ständig, so dass eine neue Art von Wohnumgebung entstanden ist, das kleine Appartement. Das mangelnde Angebot an bewohnbaren Flächen spiegelt sich in unseren Wohnungen in einer Verkleinerung des bewohnbaren Raums wider, wobei oft ein Minimum erreicht wird.

Der Grundriss kleiner Appartements ist dem normal großer Wohnungen sehr ähnlich; die winzigste Wohnung kann noch besondere Funktionen wie ein Studio oder eine Leseecke enthalten. Was diese Art von Wohnung von ihren größeren Geschwistern unterscheidet, sind die Strategien, die die Architekten und Innenarchitekten anwenden, um den vorhandenen Raum bestmöglich auszunutzen und um die architektonischen Elemente der Wohnung zu unterstreichen. Diese Appartements fallen gerade aufgrund des Einfallsreichtums auf, mit dem die notwendigen Wohnfunktionen auf kleinstem Raum untergebracht wurden, ohne dabei auf Qualität oder Bequemlichkeit für die Bewohner zu verzichten.

Viele dieser Gestaltungsstrategien sind allen Appartements gemeinsam. So wird sehr oft der gleiche Raum für verschiedene Funktionen benutzt. Innovative Strategien können Wände sein, die nicht bis zur Decke oder zu Seitenwand reichen, Schiebetüren, die verborgen werden können, mobile Schirme, mit denen man die Anordnung der Wohnung ändern kann, oder Öffnungen und durchscheinendes Material, durch das Licht in alle abgetrennten Bereiche strömen kann. Obwohl überall eine eigene, spezifische Lösung gefunden wurde, kann man doch, wenn man alle Strategien zum Ausnutzen des vorhanden Raums vergleicht, fünf Aspekte erkennen, die grundlegend für eine erfolgreiche Gestaltung und die wichtigsten Funktionen dieser Appartements sind, nämlich funktionelle Möbel, der Einsatz von Farben, bewegliche Paneele, eine gewisse Reduzierung und die äußere Umgebung.

In diesem Sammelband kleiner Appartements auf der ganzen Welt wurde ein besonderes Augenmerk auf die Besonderheiten eines jeden Raums gerichtet, innerhalb des allgemeinen Planungsproblems, das der Platzmangel aufwirft. Diese verschiedenen Projekte sind nicht nur für Architekten und Innenarchitekten interessant, sondern auch für den modernen Großstadtbewohner. Dieses Buch vermittelt das Verständnis dafür, wie Architekten, Innenarchitekten oder Eigentümer kleiner Wohnungen einen minimalen Wohnraum planen.

SMALL APARTMENTS
PETITS APPARTEMENTS
KLEINE APPARTEMENTS

Residence in Monte-Carlo
Résidence à Monte Carlo
Wohnung in Monte-Carlo

Claudio Lazzarini & Carl Pickering

The main objective of this project was to create a distinctive, continuous and fluid space which takes advantage of the magnificent views of the sea off Monte Carlo. To achieve this, the loading wall that divides the apartment lengthwise was disguised by inserting mirrors, glass shapes, and stainless-steel openings that appear to pass from one side to another. The bathroom, kitchen and closets were conceived as independent units that form part of the setting. The terrace, modelled on the deck of a ship, is an integral part of the interior. It allows the interior to expand and flow outdoors. Sunlight alters with the color of the glazed objects, intensifying and diversifying the effects of the lamps around the apartment. The glass boxes on the walls present a motley array of colors, according to the light that filters through them. The partitions are fitted with rollers so that they can be moved at will.

L'objectif principal de ce projet est de créer un espace différent, continu et fluide qui tire parti des vues splendides sur la mer, au large de Monte Carlo. A cet effet, le mur porteur qui divise l'appartement dans le sens de la longueur est orné de miroirs, serti de formes en verre et d'ouvertures en acier inoxydable qui semblent traverser l'espace. La salle de bains, la cuisine et les toilettes sont conçues en unités indépendantes faisant partie du décor. La terrasse, à l'instar d'un pont de navire, est partie intégrante de l'intérieur qu'elle agrandit et étend vers l'extérieur. La lumière du soleil joue avec les couleurs des objets vernis, intensifiant et diversifiant les effets des lampes autour de l'appartement. Les boîtes en verre sur les murs deviennent de véritables kaléidoscopes de couleurs sous l'action de l'intensité de la lumière qui les traverse. Les cloisons sont sur roulettes afin d'être déplacées au gré des besoins.

Die Gestaltungsidee war es, einen besonderen, durchgehenden und fließenden Raum zu schaffen, von dem aus man den wundervollen Blick auf die See vor Monte Carlo genießen konnte. Deshalb wurde die schwere Wand, die das Appartement der Länge nach teilt, mit Spiegeln, Formen aus Glas und Öffnungen aus Edelstahl verkleidet, die von einer Seite zur anderen zu gehen scheinen. Das Bad, die Küche und die Schränke wurden als unabhängige Einheiten angelegt, die einen Teil des Gesamtbildes darstellen. Die Terrasse, die wie ein Schiffsdeck aussieht, ist ein Bestandteil der inneren Räume, die sich über sie nach außen ausweiten. Das Sonnenlicht verändert sich durch die Farben der verglasten Objekte, es intensiviert oder zerstreut die Wirkung der Beleuchtung. Die Glaskästen an der Wand leuchten in vielen Farben, je nach dem, wie sich das Licht durch sie gefiltert wird. Die Raumteiler sind mit Rollen ausgestattet und können bewegt werden.

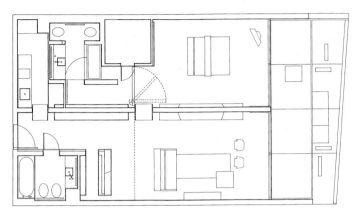

Plan Plan Grundriss

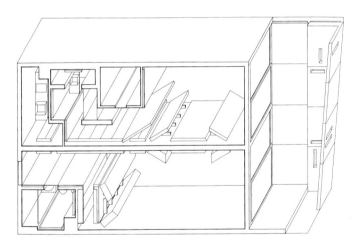

Perspective Perspective Perspektivzeichnung

The glass boxes hide the load-bearing structure.

Les boîtes en verre masquent la structure portante.

Die Glaskästen verbergen die tragende Struktur.

The glass boxes on the walls take on an array of different colors according to the light filtering through them.

Les boîtes en verre sur les murs sont de véritables kaléidoscopes de couleurs selon l'intensité de la lumière qui les traverse.

Die Glaskästen an der Wand leuchten in vielen Farben, je nach dem, wie das Licht durch sie gefiltert wird.

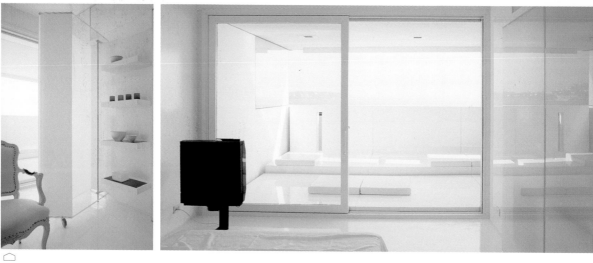

The bathroom adjoins the bedroom, while the shower is located behind the bed.

La salle de bains est adjacente à la chambre à coucher et la douche se situe derrière le lit.

Das Bad liegt neben dem Schlafzimmer und die Dusche ist hinter dem Bett platziert.

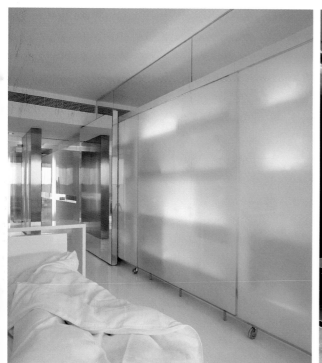

The main objective was to create a continuous, fluid space that took advantage of the magnificent views.

L'objectif principal était de créer un espace continu et fluide qui tire parti des vues splendides.

Es sollte ein durchgehender, fließender Raum geschaffen werden, von dem aus man einen wundervollen Blick hat.

Olympic Tower Residence
Résidence de la Tour Olympique
Wohnung im Olympiaturm

Gabellini Associates

This luxury apartment on the corner of the 49th floor of a building located on New York's Fifth Avenue has impressive views of the Rockefeller Center and mid-Manhattan. The design concept consisted of a bright, crystal-clear space that serves as a vantage point for the vibrant city below. The audiovisual system is contained in a structure that acts as the pivot for the distribution of the main living and dining areas and the master bedroom. The atmosphere of the interior is created with several luxury materials and a simple color scheme dominated by white plaster, marble from Yugoslavia, and translucent crystal. A glass wall formed by two white enamelled panels lit from below separates the kitchen from the dining area. The design balances the use of light, forms, and materials and allows them to coexist harmoniously in this minimalist environment.

Cet appartement luxueux, à l'angle du 49e étage d'un édifice situé sur la 5e avenue de New York, offre des vues fabuleuses sur le Centre Rockefeller et le cœur de Manhattan. La conception du design présente un espace vaste et extrêmement clair, très bien situé au-dessus de la cité vibrante. Le système audiovisuel est contenu dans une structure qui est l'axe de la distribution du salon, de la salle à manger et de la chambre à coucher principale. L'atmosphère intérieure est le fruit de divers matériaux luxueux et de l'unité de couleur créée par le plâtre blanc, le marbre de Yougoslavie et le cristal translucide. Un vitrage, formé de deux panneaux en émail blanc éclairés par le bas, sépare la cuisine de la salle à manger. Le design conjugue l'emploi des lumières, des formes et des matériaux dans un équilibre harmonieux au sein de cet univers minimaliste.

Diese luxuriöse Wohnung an der Ecke eines 49. Stockwerks in einem Gebäude an der Fifth Avenue in New York bietet einen überwältigenden Blick auf das Rockefeller Center und Mid-Manhattan. Das Gestaltungskonzept war es, einen hellen, kristallklaren Raum zu schaffen, der einen Aussichtspunkt über die vibrierende Stadt unter sich darstellt. Das audiovisuelle System ist in einer Struktur untergebracht, die den Angelpunkt für die Verteilung der wichtigsten Wohn- und Essbereiche und das Hauptschlafzimmer bildet. Das Innere ist mit luxuriösen Materialien ausgestattet, die Farben sind einfach, weißer Gips dominiert, außerdem wurden jugoslawischer Marmor und durchscheinendes Kristall verwendet. Eine Glaswand aus zwei weißen, glasierten Paneelen, die von unten beleuchtet werden, trennt die Küche vom Essbereich ab. Die Gestalter spielten mit Licht, Formen und Materialien und ließen diese Elemente harmonisch miteinander in dieser minimalistischen Umgebung zusammenfließen.

Plan Plan Grundriss

The design balances the use of light, forms, and materials.
Le design décline l'emploi des lumières, formes et matériaux dans un équilibre harmonieux
Die Raumgestaltung beruht auf dem Spiel mit Licht, Formen und Materialien.

A glass wall formed by two white enamelled panels separates the kitchen from the dining area.

Un vitrage, formé de deux panneaux en émail blanc illuminés par le bas, sépare la cuisine de la salle à manger.

Eine Glaswand aus zwei weißen, glasierten Paneelen, die von unten beleuchtet wird, trennt die Küche vom Essbereich ab.

☐ Residential Building
Bâtiment résidentiel
Wohngebäude

Paskin Kyriakides Sands

This project in the center of London included the creation of 36 residential units, including 5 penthouses, which occupy the entire top floor of this old office building. The architects, in collaboration with Philippe Stark, were awarded the commission for the design and construction of this complex in a competition. This resulted in the creation of a series of striking, modern apartments, with exquisite details and finishes, within a layout that made the most of the structural and lighting conditions that already existed. Each living unit was based on the same concept: the creation of a single, expansive space for the living areas and independent zones for the kitchen, bedroom, and bathroom. The wide range of interiors spread over the eleven floors that make up the building were enriched by the changes in level, high ceilings, and exterior terraces.

Ce projet au centre de Londres comprend la création de 36 unités industrielles, dont 5 duplex, occupant tout l'étage supérieur de ces anciens bureaux. Les architectes, en collaboration avec Philippe Stark, ont remporté le concours pour la conception du design et de la construction de ce complexe. Une série d'appartements modernes et originaux ont été construits : détails et finitions très raffinés, au sein d'un plan qui a su tirer parti de la structure et de la lumière existante. Chaque modèle de salon suit le même concept de base : la création d'un vaste espace unique pour le salon et de zones indépendantes pour la cuisine, la chambre à coucher et la salle de bains. Le grand éventail d'intérieurs déployé sur les onze étages du bâtiment est enrichi par des différences de niveaux, des hauts plafonds et des terrasses extérieures.

Dieses Bauvorhaben im Zentrum von London umfasste die Schaffung von 36 Wohnungen, darunter 5 Dachterrassenwohnungen, die das ganze obere Stockwerk des ehemaligen Bürogebäudes einnehmen. Die Architekten erhielten zusammen mit Philippe Stark bei einer Ausschreibung den Auftrag für die Gestaltung und den Bau dieses Komplexes. Sie schufen eine Reihe von bemerkenswerten modernen Appartements mit außergewöhnlich schönen Einzelheiten und Materialien und einer Raumaufteilung, die das Beste aus den vorhandenen Strukturelementen und dem Tageslicht macht. Jede Wohnung beruht auf dem gleichen Konzept, die Schaffung eines einzigen, weiten Raums für die Wohnbereiche und unabhängige Zonen für die Küche, Schlafzimmer und Bad. Die verschiedenen Räume in den elf Stockwerken wurden noch durch die Konstruktion verschiedener Ebenen, hoher Decken und Terrassen im Freien verschönert.

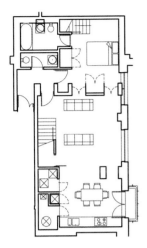

Plan Plan Grundriss

Elevations Élévations Aufrisse

First floor Premier étage Erstes Obergeschoss

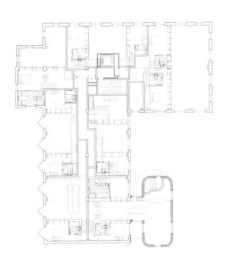

Ground floor Rez-de-chaussée Erdgeschoss

The combination of the wooden floor, glass and metal adds up to a unique, modern setting.

L'alliance du parquet, du verre et du métal exalte le caractère unique et moderne de cet agencement.

Durch die Kombination des Holzbodens mit Glas und Metall entstand eine einzigartige, moderne Wohnlandschaft.

The building's original structure was ideal for creating urban living spaces on multiple levels.

La structure d'origine du bâtiment est idéale pour y créer des logements urbains sur différents niveaux.

Die Originalstruktur des Gebäudes eignete sich ideal für die Schaffung städtischer Wohnungen auf verschiedenen Ebenen.

single space was created for the living areas while the kitchen, bedroom, and bathroom were separated off.

e salon occupe un espace unique contrairement à la cuisine, la chambre à coucher et la salle de bains qui sont des espaces séparés.

s wurde ein einziger Raum für die Wohnbereiche geschaffen, während die Küche, das Schlafzimmer und das Bad separat liegen.

Horizontal Unit
Unité horizontale
Waagerechte Einheit

Stephen Quinn & Elise Ovanessoff

This apartment is located on the first floor of a typical four-story Georgian house in the Marylebone neighborhood. The apartment consisted of two different settings connected by some steps. The architects first restored the large room at the front to its former size and moved the kitchen to a more convenient location. The bedroom is set to the rear and leads to a walk-in closet with a sliding door painted with green and blue stripes. The bathroom was carefully designed to cater to all the clients' needs. All the walls are white and the decorative elements are limited to objects, sculptures, and statuettes placed on top of tables. Some features, such as the fireplace and large windows, evoke the spirit of the old house. A crucial characteristic of this project is the use of space and light, which, combined with the high ceilings, transforms this small apartment into a modern and practical home.

Cet appartement est situé au premier étage d'une maison géorgienne typique, à quatre étages, dans le quartier Marylebone. L'appartement présente deux espaces différents reliés par quelques marches. Les architectes ont d'abord restauré la grande pièce à l'avant de la maison en la ramenant à sa taille d'origine et déplacé la cuisine à un meilleur endroit. La chambre à coucher se situe à l'arrière et mène à un dressing doté d'une porte coulissante peinte de rayures vertes et bleues. La salle de bains a été conçue avec un soin particulier pour répondre à tous les besoins du client. Les murs sont blancs et la décoration se limite à quelques objets, sculptures et statuettes posés sur des tables. Certains éléments, à l'instar de la cheminée et des grandes fenêtres, rappellent l'esprit de l'ancienne maison. La caractéristique essentielle de ce projet est de jongler avec l'utilisation de l'espace, de la lumière et la hauteur des plafonds pour transformer ce petit appartement en une maison pratique et moderne.

Diese Wohnung befindet sich im ersten Stock eines typischen, vierstöckigen, georgianischen Hauses in Marylebone. Sie besteht aus zwei verschiedenen Ebenen, die über einige Stufen miteinander verbunden sind. Die Architekten gaben zunächst dem großen, vorderen Raum seine ursprüngliche Größe zurück und verlegten die Küche an einen besseren Ort. Das Schlafzimmer liegt hinten und führt zu einem begehbaren Kleiderschrank mit einer Schiebetür, die mit grünen und blauen Streifen gestrichen ist. Das sorgfältig gestaltete Badezimmer integriert alle notwendigen Funktionen. Alle Wände sind weiß und die einzigen Dekorationselemente sind Objekte, Skulpturen und Statuen auf den Tischen. Einige Elemente wie der Kamin und die großen Fenster beschwören den Geist der alten Zeit herauf. Wichtigstes Merkmal dieser Raumgestaltung ist die Art und Weise, wie Raum und Licht eingesetzt werden, die in Kombination mit den hohen Decken aus dieser kleinen Wohnung ein modernes und funktionelles Zuhause machen.

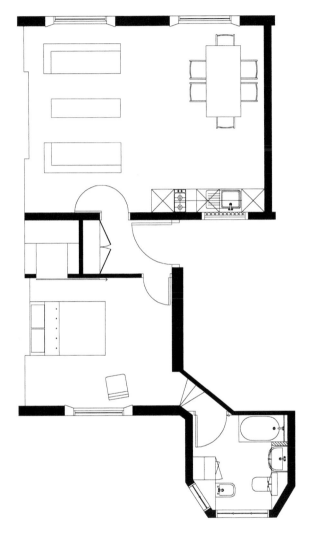

Plan Plan Grundriss

A crucial characteristic of this project is the use of space and light.

La caractéristique essentielle de ce projet est de jongler avec l'utilisation de l'espace et de la lumière.

Wichtigstes Merkmal dieser Raumgestaltung ist die Art und Weise, wie Raum und Licht eingesetzt werden.

The bedroom is set to the rear and leads to a walk-in closet.

La chambre à coucher se situe à l'arrière et mène à un dressing.

Das Schlafzimmer liegt hinten versetzt und führt zu einem begehbaren Kleiderschrank.

All the walls are white and the decorative elements are limited to objects, sculptures, and statuettes placed on top of tables.

Les murs sont blancs et la décoration se limite à quelques objets, sculptures et statuettes posés sur des tables.

Alle Wände sind weiß und die einzigen Dekorationselemente sind die Objekte, Skulpturen und Statuetten auf den Tischen.

☐ House in La Azohía
Maison à La Azohía
Haus in La Azohía

José Tarragó

The inner rooms of this home are entirely permeable from the visual point of view: interrelated and open toward the exterior, they allow no introspection of any kind. In contrast, the patios are conceived as interiors: they are precincts enclosed by walls that isolate them from the surrounding landscape. Outdoors, the home incorporates elements of traditional architecture that protect it from bad weather: thick walls provide thermal insulation, whitewash reflects the sun's rays, and the openings have been inserted in shady spots, wherever possible. On the other hand, the interior—including the patios—has a contemporary, almost futuristic, feel. The furniture combines white with a wide range of ochers, and includes exclusive, one-off pieces. The kitchen opens on to the living room, which is characterized by pure lines, formal restraint, and the smooth, spotless white surfaces of the closets.

Sur le plan visuel, les espaces intérieurs de cette maison sont totalement transparents : reliés à l'extérieur sur lequel ils s'ouvrent, ils jouissent d'une transparence totale. En contraste, les patios sont conçus comme des intérieurs : ils sont entourés de murs qui les coupent du paysage environnant. A l'extérieur, la maison intègre des éléments d'architecture traditionnelle qui la protègent des intempéries : murs épais pour l'isolation thermique, blanchis à la chaux pour refléter les rayons de soleil et ouvertures placées dans des endroits ombragés, tant que faire se peut. En opposition, l'intérieur – les patios y compris – dégage une impression contemporaine, presque futuriste. Le mobilier décline le blanc et une grande palette d'ocres et se distingue par l'exclusivité de ses pièces uniques. La cuisine s'ouvre sur le salon, caractérisé par la pureté des lignes, la sobriété des formes et la douceur des surfaces blanches et immaculées des placards.

Die Räume dieser Wohnung sind visuell absolut durchlässig, sie stehen miteinander in Verbindung und öffnen sich nach außen, man kann nicht nach innen blicken. Im Gregensatz dazu werden, die Höfe wie Innenräume behandelt, sie sind Zonen, die von Wänden eingeschlossen sind, die sie von der umgebenden Landschaft abtrennen. An der Fassade des Hauses befinden sich traditionelle, architektonische Elemente, die vor schlechtem Wetter schützen. Dicke Wände sorgen für eine Wärmeisolierung, weiße Tünche reflektiert die Sonnenstrahlen und die Fenster wurden soweit wie möglich an schattigen Stellen konstruiert. Im Gegensatz dazu wirkt das Innere einschließlich der Höfe sehr zeitgemäß, fast futuristisch. Die Möbel kombinieren Weiß mit verschiedenen Ockertönen, zum Teil handelt es sich um exklusive Einzelanfertigungen. Die Küche öffnet sich zum Wohnzimmer, in dem klare Linien, zurückhaltende Formen und die glatte, einheitlich weiße Oberfläche der Wandschränke vorherrschen.

The patios are precincts enclosed by walls that isolate them from the surrounding landscape.

Les patios sont entourés de murs qui les coupent du paysage environnant.

Die Höfe sind von Mauern eingeschlossen, die sie von der umgebenden Landschaft abtrennen.

The openings on the facade, the skylights, and the colors on the furniture bestow a sense of luminosity on the dwelling.

Les ouvertures en façade, les velux et les couleurs des meubles exaltent la sensation de luminosité de la demeure.

Die Fassadenfenster, die Dachfenster und die Farben der Möbel lassen diese Wohnung sehr hell wirken.

Apartment in London
Appartement à Londres
Appartement in London

Blockarchitecture

The aim of the renovation of this loft was to allow the concrete and brick structure that defines and enshrouds the entire space to be as complete and open as possible. A thirty-foot wall built of recycled steel panels dominates and organizes the residence by defining a hall, a small storeroom, a bathroom separate from the toilet, and a photographer´s darkroom. The remaining household functions, including the kitchen and bath, are located alongside the opposite wall. The shower and bathroom occupy a special position, raised on a platform of concrete that floats above the wooden floor. The area has no partition walls or curtains, demonstrating an unconventional approach to the privacy of bathroom space. While some walls and structural columns were restored, many were left exposed and intact. Their rough, sparsely plastered brick surfaces create an informal but stylish environment. The walls themselves are decorative objects that give an industrial character to the loft space.

La rénovation de ce loft prévoyait l'ouverture totale de la structure en béton et briques définissant et encadrant l'ensemble de l'espace. Un mur de 9 m, construit à base de panneaux recyclés, structure et domine la résidence. Il définit un hall, un petit espace de rangement, une salle de bains avec toilettes séparées et une chambre noire. Les autres fonctions domestiques, la cuisine et une salle de douche se situent le long du mur opposé. La douche et la salle de bains, installées sur une plate-forme de béton flottant au-dessus du parquet, occupent une place particulière. Dépourvues de cloisons, de murs ou de rideaux, elles traduisent une notion inhabituelle de l'intimité dans une salle d'eau. Certains murs et piliers structuraux ont été restaurés, mais beaucoup ont été laissés apparents et intacts. Leur revêtement rugueux, parsemé de briques, donne du style à cet environnement informel. Les murs font aussi partie du décor conférant à ce loft un caractère industriel.

Ziel der Renovierung dieses Lofts war es, mit der Beton- und Ziegelstruktur den gesamten Raum so vollständig und offen wie möglich zu definieren und umgeben. Eine 9 Meter lange Wand aus recycelten Stahlplatten beherrscht und organisiert die Wohnung. Sie definiert den Flur, die kleine Abstellkammer, das von der Toilette getrennte Bad und die Dunkelkammer. Die übrigen Funktionen sowie Küche und Bad befinden sich entlang der gegenüberliegenden Wand. Die Dusche und das Badezimmer nehmen einen besonderen Platz ein, sie stehen auf einer Betonplattform über dem Holzfußboden. Es gibt keine Trennwände oder Gardinen, so wird auf unkonventionelle Art Privatsphäre im Bad geschaffen. Manche der Wände und Säulen des Gebäudes wurden restauriert, viele sind sichtbar und intakt. Die rauhen, kaum verputzten Backsteinoberflächen schaffen eine zwanglose und dennoch stilvolle Atmosphäre. Die Wände selbst sind die Dekorationsobjekte, die dem Loft einen industriellen Charakter verleihen.

While some walls and structural columns were restored, many were left exposed and intact.

Certains murs et piliers structuraux ont été restaurés, mais beaucoup ont été laissés apparents et intacts.

Manche der Wände und Säulen des Gebäudes wurden restauriert, viele sind sichtbar und intakt.

☐ Dwelling in New Jersey
Maison à New Jersey
Residenz in New Jersey

Barbara De Vries & Alastair Gordon

A fashion designer and a writer discovered this building and decided to convert it into a place to live and work. The clients wanted to preserve certain elements and adapt them to their lifestyle: the industrial look, the brick walls, the immense windows, the open ceiling, and the cement floor. Metal elements support the wooden structure, which looks like a house inside a house; this approach divides the space while maintaining the original atmosphere. The small living area is separated from the rest of the rooms by birch-wood panels on rails, so that the space can be enlarged or closed off at will. The sparse furnishings further emphasize the industrial aspect and the feeling of open space. To create a more intimate and warm atmosphere, the designers used pieces of furniture and natural materials. The settings are separated by translucent panels, thus allowing the natural light entering through the large windows to bathe every corner of the home.

En découvrant cette construction, un designer de mode et un écrivain ont décidé de la convertir en lieu de vie et de travail. A la requête des clients, certains éléments ont été conservés et adapter à leur style de vie : l'aspect industriel, les murs en briques, les fenêtres immenses, le plafond ouvert et le sol en ciment. Les éléments de métal qui soutiennent l'ossature en bois donnent l'impression d'une maison dans une maison. Cette approche permet de diviser l'espace tout en gardant l'atmosphère d'origine. La zone du petit salon est séparée du reste des pièces par des cloisons en bois de bouleau montées sur rails, ouvrant ou fermant l'espace au gré des besoins. La parcimonie du mobilier exalte l'aspect industriel et la sensation d'espace ouvert. Pour créer une atmosphère plus chaleureuse et intime les designers ont utilisé certains meubles et des matériaux naturels. Les différents espaces sont séparés par des panneaux translucides laissant la lumière naturelle des grandes fenêtres inonder les moindres coins et recoins de l'appartement.

Zwei Menschen, die sich dem Modedesign und dem Schreiben widmen, entdeckten dieses Haus und es sollte ihr Wohn- und Arbeitsort werden. Bestimmte Elemente blieben erhalten und wurden an ihren Lebensstil angepasst, wie z. B. das industrielle Aussehen, die Ziegelwände, die riesigen Fenster, das offene Dach und der Zementboden. Metallelemente stützen die Holzstruktur, die wie ein Haus in einem Haus wirkt. So wird der Raum unterteilt, ohne an Atmosphäre einzubüßen. Das kleine Wohnzimmer ist von den übrigen Räumen durch Birkenholzpaneele auf Schienen abgetrennt, so dass es vergrößert oder abgetrennt werden kann. Die spärliche Möblierung unterstreicht das industrielle Aussehen und das Gefühl von Weite. Mit bestimmten Möbelstücken und natürlichen Materialien wird eine warme, einladende Atmosphäre geschaffen. Die Bereiche sind mit durchscheinenden Paneelen voneinander getrennt, so dass das Tageslicht durch die riesigen Fenster in jeden Winkel einfallen kann.

To create a more intimate and warm atmosphere, the designers used pieces of furniture and natural materials.

Pour créer une atmosphère plus chaleureuse et intime les designers ont utilisé certains meubles et des matériaux naturels.

Mit bestimmten Möbelstücken und natürlichen Materialien wird eine warme, einladende Atmosphäre geschaffen.

☐ Residence in Gracia
Résidence à Gracia
Wohnung in Gracia

Sandra Aparicio + Forteza Carbonell Associats

This residential project consisted of renovating the upper level of an old industrial building with a pitched roof. The original space had a large ground floor and a small top floor with access to a terrace. The main aims were to flood the space with natural light and create some spacious rooms. A large skylight was installed over the living and dining areas while other smaller openings were inserted to cast light on the bathrooms. The framework crossing the large, central skylight causes the light to reflect in several directions, creating an environment that changes throughout the day. The layout of the space is organized around a furniture element that separates the night area from the day area. It does not reach as far as the ceiling or the apartment's exterior walls, thus emphasizing the fluidity of the space. The piece serves as a shelf on the communal side and a closet on the private side.

Ce projet de résidence concerne la rénovation de l'étage supérieur d'un ancien bâtiment au toit élevé. La découpe originale de base offrait un grand rez-de-chaussée et un petit étage supérieur avec accès à la terrasse. Le but essentiel du nouveau projet était d'inonder l'espace de lumière naturelle et de créer des grandes pièces. Un grand velux a donc été installé au-dessus du salon et de la salle à manger, des ouvertures plus petites ont été créées pour éclairer la salle de bains. Le grand velux central est doté d'une structure qui a pour effet de réfléchir la lumière dans diverses directions, créant une ambiance qui varie au fil de la journée. L'espace s'articule autour d'une pièce de mobilier qui sépare la zone de jour de la zone de nuit. Il n'atteint ni le plafond ni les murs extérieurs, renforçant ainsi la fluidité de l'espace. Ce meuble sert d'étagères du côté jour et d'armoire du côté privé.

Dieses Bauvorhaben umfasste die Renovierung des oberen Stockwerks eines alten Industriegebäudes mit einem geneigten Dach. In diesem Gebäude gab es einst ein großes Erdgeschoss und eine kleine obere Etage mit Zugang zur Terrasse. Hauptziel der Planung war es, die Räumlichkeiten mit Tageslicht zu füllen und große Räume zu schaffen. Über dem Wohn- und Essbereich wurde ein großes Dachfenster geschaffen, und kleinere Fenster wurden geöffnet, um Licht ins Bad zu lassen. Das Licht wird von den Rahmen, die das große, zentrale Dachfenster durchkreuzen, reflektiert und schafft so eine Umgebung, die sich je nach Tageszeit verändert. Der Raum ist um ein Möbelelement organisiert, das den Bereich für die Nacht von dem für den Tag trennt. Es reicht nicht bis zur Decke oder zu den Außenwänden, um den Raum nicht zu unterbrechen. Dieses Element dient als Regal im Wohnbereich und als Schrank im Schlafbereich.

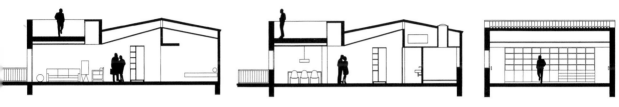

ctions Sections Schnitte

Ground floor Rez-de-chaussée Erdgeschoss

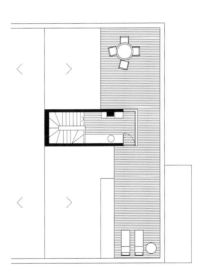

First floor Premier étage Erstes Obergeschoss

The main aims were to flood the space with natural light and create spacious rooms.

Le but essentiel du nouveau projet était de créer de grands espaces et de les inonder de lumière naturelle.

Hauptziel der Planung war es, die Räumlichkeiten mit Tageslicht zu füllen und große Räume zu schaffen.

A large skylight was installed over the living area, while other smaller openings illuminate the bathrooms.

Un grand velux a donc été installé au-dessus du salon et de la salle à manger, des ouvertures plus petites illuminent la salle de bains.

Ein großes Dachfenster über dem Wohnbereich und kleinere Fenster in den Badezimmern lassen Tageslicht in die Räume.

☐ London Mews

Co-labarchitects

For this project, the client wanted to create a private residence by combining two typical commercial mews in London. The restrictions of the façade and the lack of any space around the property called for a strategy that consisted of opening up the rear of the building as much as possible and creating light, subtle barriers inside. This approach created a space that was open, ventilated, and well lit. Several skylights, as well as a few carefully placed interior mirrors, brighten the space and make it feel even more open. The remodelling also created a more cohesive composition than the previous series of subdivided spaces, which were different in character from each other. Most of the interior walls were removed and a common language was created, based on the consistent use of materials and finishings throughout the two units. The rich color and texture of the materials create a soft, warm atmosphere that is more suited to the new residential function.

Dans ce projet, le client voulait créer une résidence privée en intégrant deux écuries converties en habitation commerciales à Londres. Les restrictions de la façade et le manque d'espace autour de la propriété ont nécessité l'application d'une stratégie adéquate : ouvrir au maximum l'arrière du bâtiment et créer un cloisonnement léger et judicieux à l'intérieur. Grâce à cette approche, l'espace a gagné en ouverture, ventilation et lumière. Divers velux, associés à des miroirs intérieurs placés à des endroits précis, élargissent le volume et donnent une sensation d'ouverture. Le remodelage spatial permet un agencement plus harmonieux que dans les anciennes pièces, plus divisées et très différentes les unes des autres. La plupart des murs intérieurs ont été supprimés. Le langage conceptuel est commun aux deux unités, employant des matériaux et finitions identiques. Les matériaux riches en couleurs et textures créent une atmosphère douce et chaleureuse plus appropriée aux nouvelles fonctions résidentielles.

Zwei typische Läden in London sollten zu einer Privatwohnung umgebaut werden. An der Fassade durften keine Eingriffe vorgenommen werden, und es war sehr wenig Platz vorhanden, so dass die Gestalter das Gebäude hinten so weit wie möglich öffneten und leichte, raffinierte Barrieren im Inneren schufen. So entstand ein offener, luftiger und heller Raum. Die Räumlichkeiten werden durch mehrere Dachfenster und strategisch verteilte Spiegel erhellt, was sie noch offener wirken lässt. Durch den Umbau entstand eine zusammenhängendere Anordnung, denn vorher war die Wohnung in einzelne Zimmer unterteilt, die alle sehr unterschiedlich waren. Die meisten Innenwände wurden entfernt und es entstand ein gemeinsamer Stil, der auf dem konsequenten Gebrauch von Materialien und Oberflächen in beiden Einheiten basiert. Durch die warmen Farben und Texturen der Materialien entsteht eine angenehme und einladende Atmosphäre, in der es sich angenehm wohnen lässt.

Ground floor Rez-de-chaussée Erdgeschoss   First floor Premier étage Erstes Obergeschoss

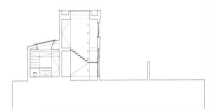

Sections Sections Schnitte

Elevations Élévations Aufrisse

The rich colors and texture of the materials create a soothing, warm atmosphere.

Les matériaux hauts en couleurs et de textures riches créent une atmosphère douce et chaleureuse.

Durch die warmen Farben und Texturen der Materialien entsteht eine angenehme und gemütliche Atmosphäre.

Various skylights brighten the space up and make it feel even more open.
Divers velux agrandissent l'espace et accentuent l'impression d'ouverture.
Der Raum wird durch mehrere Dachfenster erhellt und wirkt so noch weiter.

Apartment in Paris
Appartement à Paris
Appartement in Paris

Peter Tyberghien

This apartment is located in Paris's 9th arrondissement, close to Montmartre and only minutes from the city center. An initial study of the space and the clients' needs led to a renovation involving the opening up of the space and elimination of the walls separating the kitchen from the rest of the apartment. This created the sensation of a larger area while making the kitchen more hospitable. The bathroom was expanded and the toilet was set apart. The metal beam running across the interior was used to divide the space into two long halves, as well as supporting a rail with track lights that supply most of the illumination. A long unit on the wall opposite the windows conceals a column that once broke up the space. This unit now serves as a bookcase, display cabinet, and closet. The wooden floor is complemented by austere furniture, while the soft, warm colors and drapes with a natural look give the apartment a cozy feel.

Cet appartement est situé à Paris, dans le 9e arrondissement, près de Montmartre et à quelques minutes du centre de la cité. L'étude initiale de l'espace et la prise en considération des besoins du client ont abouti à la restauration de l'espace : ouverture des volumes et suppression des murs séparant la cuisine du reste de l'appartement. L'espace semble ainsi plus généreux et la cuisine plus accueillante. La salle de bains a été agrandie et les toilettes séparées. La poutre de métal traversant l'intérieur, divise l'espace en deux longues moitiés et sert d'appui à un rail de lumière qui fournit presque tout l'éclairage de la pièce. Un long module mural, face au côté fenêtre, masque une colonne qui divisait l'espace antérieur. Il abrite maintenant des étagères de livres, une vitrine et une armoire. Le plancher est associé à des meubles austères. Couleurs douces et chaudes et tentures naturelles confèrent à l'appartement un caractère accueillant et convivial.

Dieses Appartement befindet sich im 9. Arondissement von Paris, in der Nähe des Montmartre und nur wenige Minuten vom Zentrum entfernt. Eine anfängliche Studie der Wohnung und der Bedürfnisse der Kunden führte dazu, dass der Raum geöffnet und die Wände, die die Küche vom Rest der Wohnung abtrennten, entfernt wurden. So wurde die Küche wohnlicher und der Raum wirkt größer. Das Badezimmer wurde vergrößert und die Toilette abgetrennt. Der Metallträger, der durch den Raum läuft, wurde zur Aufteilung des Raumes in zwei Hälften benutzt und als Träger für eine Schiene, an der fast die gesamte Beleuchtung angebracht ist. Eine lange Einheit an der den Fenstern gegenüberliegenden Wand verbirgt eine Säule, die den Raum einst teilte. Diese Einheit dient als Bücherschrank, Vitrine und Wandschrank. Der Holzfußboden ergänzt die einfachen Möbel und weiche, warme Farben und Naturstoffe sorgen für Gemütlichkeit.

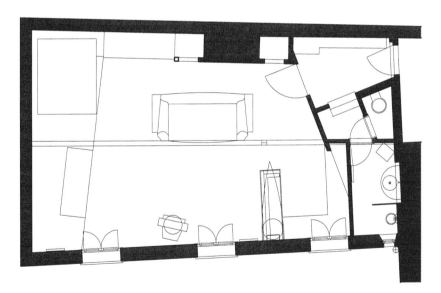

Planta Pianta Planta

The wooden floor is complemented by austere furniture, while the soft, warm colors and drapes with a natural look give the apartment a cozy feel.

Le plancher est associé à des meubles austères. Couleurs douces et chaudes et tentures naturelles confèrent à l'appartement un caractère accueillant et convivial.

Der Holzfußboden ergänzt die einfachen Möbel und weiche, warme Farben und Naturstoffe sorgen für Gemütlichkeit.

Residence in Bogota
Résidence à Bogota
Wohnung in Bogota

Luis Cuartas

Two architects transformed this space into their personal residence. After demolishing the existing walls, the architects laid out the new spaces that make up the residence. The aim was to create a continual space with multiple relationships between the different areas, and a continuous, circular path that joins up the entire home. There are two alternative routes. On the left, a table extends all the way to the door and invites visitors to enter the kitchen. On the right, a corridor containing a large bench and a bathroom integrated with the fireplace leads to the living room, which features unexpectedly high ceilings. From here, a steel staircase leads to a walkway to a small studio linked to a terrace. The steel and glass structure of the walkway creates an impression of lightness, while the walls that make up the interior volumes add a feeling of solidity.

Deux architectes ont modifié cette espace situé pour en faire leur résidence personnelle. Une fois les murs préexistants démolis, les architectes ont conçu les nouveaux espaces de leur résidence selon certains critères : fluidité, relations multiples entre les diverses zones et un passage continu et circulaire, fil d'Ariane de l'appartement, avec deux variantes possibles. A gauche, une table allant jusqu'à la porte invite à entrer dans la cuisine. A droite, un couloir doté d'un long banc, d'une salle de bains et d'une cheminée intégrée, mène au salon sous une hauteur de plafond inattendue. De là, un escalier d'acier conduit à une passerelle vers un petit bureau relié à une terrasse. La structure d'acier et de verre de la passerelle crée une impression de légèreté, contrastant avec les murs qui renforcent la sensation de solidité des volumes intérieurs.

Zwei Architekten bauten diese Räume zu ihrer eigenen Wohnung um. Nachdem die vorhandenen Wände niedergerissen waren, wurden die Räume neu verteilt. Es sollte ein durchgehender Raum entstehen, in dem die verschiedenen Bereiche miteinander in Beziehung stehen, und ein durchgehender Rundweg sollte alles miteinander verbinden. Es gibt zwei verschiedene Wege, links erstreckt sich der Tisch bis zur Tür und lädt den Besucher dazu ein, die Küche zu betreten. Auf der rechten Seite befindet sich ein Korridor mit einer langen Bank und ein Badezimmer, das mit dem Kamin verbunden ist. Hier geht es zum Wohnzimmer mit seiner ungewöhnlich hohen Decke. Dann führt eine Stahltreppe weiter zu einem Laufsteg, der zu dem kleine Studio führt, an dem sich die Terrasse befindet. Die Stahl- und Glasstruktur des Laufstegs erweckt das Gefühl von Leichtigkeit, während die Wände der inneren Volumen Festigkeit vermitteln.

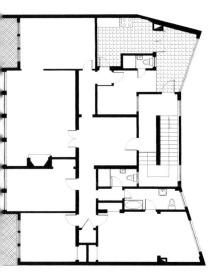

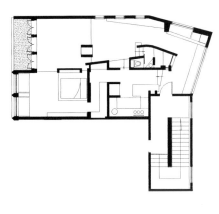

Plans Plans Grundrisse

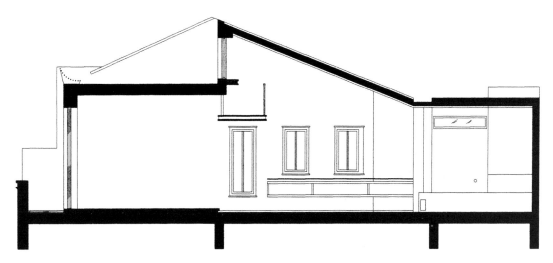

Cross section Section transversale Querschnitt

The apartment's interior configuration allows the path to cross all the spaces, taking advantage of the available space while also marking off the different settings.

La configuration de l'intérieur de l'appartement permet au passage de traverser tout l'espace tirant parti de l'espace disponible tout en délimitant les divers agencements.

Der Raum wird von einem Flur durchzogen, der den zur Verfügung stehenden Platz nutzt und die verschiedenen Bereiche unterteilt.

Concrete, green marble, brick, wood, steel, and glass combine harmoniously to give each space its own personality.

Béton, marbre vert, briques, bois, acier et verre se mélangent harmonieusement pour imprimer à chaque espace son caractère propre.

Beton, grüner Marmor, Ziegelstein, Holz, Stahl und Glas in harmonischer Kombination verleihen jedem Raum einen eigenen Charakter.

Apartment in Soho
Appartement à Soho
Appartement in Soho

Procter & Rihl

This apartment originally consisted of a studio linked by a staircase to the bedroom and the terrace. The spaces were badly designed, due to the awkward positioning of the stairs and the excessive size of the terrace in comparison to the apartment. The interior space was extended upward and outward to provide views over the east and west of London. The layout of the apartment was inverted, placing the kitchen and living room on the upper floor while relocating the bedroom, entrance, bathroom, and studio on the ground floor. The space was made to look larger through the strategic location of mirrors and, similarly, the definition of details contributed to the sensation of greater expansiveness. The definition of space has been achieved subtly by using of contrasting textures, without any need to separate the rooms, so a wide variety of materials have been used inside the apartment.

Cet appartement était au départ un bureau relié à la chambre à coucher et à la terrasse par un escalier. Il y avait une mauvaise configuration de l'espace due à l'emplacement mal choisi de l'escalier et de la taille excessive de la terrasse par rapport au reste de l'appartement. L'espace intérieur a donc été agrandi vers le haut et vers l'extérieur ouvrant ainsi la vue sur l'est et l'ouest de Londres. Le plan de base a été inversé, avec la cuisine et le salon à l'étage supérieur et la chambre à coucher, l'entrée, la salle de bains et le bureau au rez-de-chaussée. Des miroirs, placés à des points stratégiques, ont permis l'agrandissement visuel de l'espace. La conception de certains détails a également exalté cette impression d'espace. La définition de l'espace est le fruit d'une exploitation judicieuse du contraste entre diverses textures sans avoir à recourir à une séparation fixe des pièces grâce à la richesse de la gamme de tissus décorant l'appartement.

Diese Wohnung war ursprünglich ein Studio, das über eine Treppe mit dem Schlafzimmer und der Terrasse verbunden war. Der Platz war unvorteilhaft aufgeteilt, da die Treppe ein ungünstige Position hatte und die Terrasse im Vergleich zur Wohnung sehr groß war. Die Räume wurden also nach oben und außen erweitert, so dass man einen Blick über den Osten und Westen Londons hat. Die Aufteilung der Wohnung wurde umgekehrt, indem Küche und Wohnzimmer in das obere Stockwerk verlegt wurden, und das Schlafzimmer, der Eingang, das Badezimmer und das Studio ins Erdgeschoss. Durch strategisch verteilte Spiegel wirkt der Raum größer und auch verschiedene, dekorative Einzelheiten tragen zum Gefühl von mehr Weite bei. Der Raum wurde sehr subtil durch die unterschiedlichen Texturen der vielfältigen Materialien definiert, ohne dass man dazu wirkliche Raumteiler benötigte.

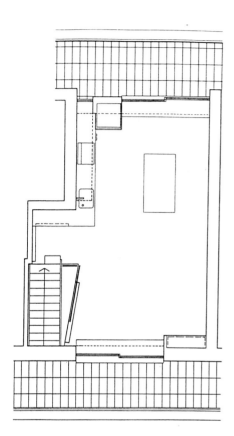

Ground floor Rez-de-chaussée Erdgeschoss

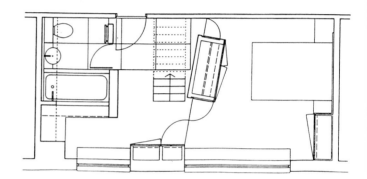

First floor Premier étage Erstes Obergeschoss

The custom-designed tables were conceived as delicate interior elements.

Les tables faites sur mesure sont des éléments subtils de décor intérieur.

Die maßgefertigten Tische werder als zierliche, innere Elemente aufgefasst.

The frameless glass windows that occupy the full height of the apartment allow for a great affluence of natural light.

L'absence d'encadrement de quelques fenêtres embrassant toute la dimension verticale laisse affluer la lumière naturelle en abondance.

Da die Fenster entlang der Längsseite des Appartements keine Fensterrahmen haben, kann das Tageslicht direkt einfallen.

The space has been subtly defined through the use of contrasting materials.

Subtile définition de l'espace grâce à des matériaux contrasté

Der Raum wird subtil durch kontrastierende Materialien unterteilt.

☐ 3R House
Maison 3R
3R Haus

Hiroyuki Arima

Although the exterior was left unaltered, the interior of this apartment was modified by eliminating fixed partitions in order to generate a continuous, open space. The name alludes to the three movable panels placed near the entrance to the apartment. By folding them at different angles, the space can be modified to provide many different combinations, depending on the needs and tastes of each resident. The floors, walls, and ceilings were painted white to enhance the low-intensity light entering from the north. The rooms succeed each other on both floors, which are linked by a staircase. The original windows have been screened by translucent plastic panels, forming small spaces that may be used for storage, as a library area, or as a belvedere overlooking the garden.

La réforme de cet appartement n'a pas compris la modification de l'extérieur. Par contre, à l'interieur il y a eu des importants modifications. Le nouveau design est conçu comme un espace fluide sans aucune cloison fixe. Le nom fait référence aux trois panneaux mobiles placés près de l'entrée de l'appartement. En les pliant selon des angles différents, on peut moduler l'espace de diverses façons, au gré des besoins et des goûts de chaque habitant. Les sols et les plafonds sont peints en blanc pour exalter la faible lumière venant du nord. Les pièces se succèdent sur les deux étages reliés par un escalier. Des panneaux translucides sont placés devant les fenêtres d'origine, pour former de petits espaces utilisés comme cagibi, bibliothèque ou encore comme balcon au-dessus du jardin.

Beim Umbau dieses Appartements wurde die äussere Struktur nicht angetastet, im Inneren dagegen jedoch bedeutende Veränderungen vorgenommen. Das Design ist durch einen durchgängingen Raum ohne feste Raumteiler gekennzeichnet. Der Name spielt auf die drei beweglichen Paneele in der Nähe des Eingangs an. Wenn man diese in verschiedene Winkel faltet, wird der Raum verändert und den Bedürfnissen und Geschmack des jeweiligen Bewohners angepasst. Böden und Decken sind weiß gestrichen, um das wenige Tageslicht, das von Norden einfällt, zu verstärken. Die Räume folgen einander auf beiden Etagen, die mit einer Treppe verbunden sind. An den Fenstern wurde ein Schirm aus durchsichtigem Kunststoff eingezogen, durch den kleine Räume entstanden, die man z. B. als Bibliothek oder Erker mit Blick auf den Garten benutzen kann.

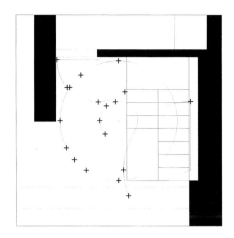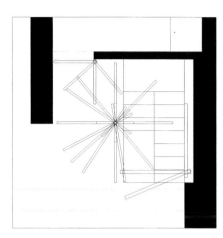

Plans Plans Grundrisse

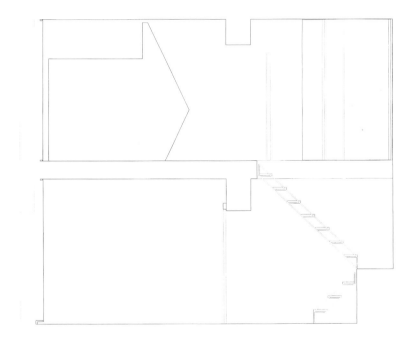

Section Section Schnitt

The rooms succeed each other on both floors, which are linked by a metal staircase.

Enfilade de pièces sur les deux étages reliés entre eux par un escalier de métal.

Die Räume folgen einander auf beiden Etagen, die mit einer Treppe verbunden sind.

The original windows have been screened by translucent plastic panels that form small spaces suitable for storage.

Des panneaux translucides ont été placés devant les fenêtres d'origine pour former de petits espaces utilisés comme cagibis.

Die ursprünglichen Fenster wurden mit durchscheinenden Kunststoffpaneelen abgeschirmt, die kleine Vorratsräume formen.

Il Hiroyuki Arima's projects reflect a typically Japanese sensitivity, a combination between tradition and futurism.

ous les projets de Hiroyuki Arima reflètent une sensibilité typiquement japonaise ou l'alliance entre la tradition et le futurisme.

lle Projekte von Hiroyuki Arima zeigen ein typisch japanisches Feingefühl, eine Mischung aus Tradition und Futurismus.

The space can be modified by folding the three movable panels that are placed near the entrance at different angles.

Il est possible de modifier l'espace en pliant les trois panneaux amovibles et en les plaçant près de l'entrée à des angles différents.

Der Raum kann durch das Falten verschiedener Winkel mit drei beweglichen Paneelen am Eingang verändert werden.

Apartment in Prenzlauer Berg
Appartement à Prenzlauer Berg
Appartement in Prenzlauer Berg

Grollmitz-Zappe

Situated on the third floor of a late-nineteenth-century industrial brick building, this flat takes full advantage of its primary construction element. Wrapped in red brick walls, a vaulted brick ceiling, and a polished cement floor, the apartment stands out for its minimal yet striking design. In the center of the space lies an unconventional bathroom pod held within a sculpted metal wire mesh, whose translucency varies according to the light it receives. The bathroom and living area occupy one half of the space, while the other half is taken up by the kitchen and dining area. Three separate, mobile kitchen units make it possible to transform a cooking space into an informal eating area. To assure the authenticity of the materials and emphasize their esthetic potential, all the electrical wiring, sockets, switches, and heating were set in the cement floor.

Situé au troisième étage d'un bâtiment industriel en briques, construit à la fin du XIXe siècle, cet appartement a optimalisé tous les éléments d'origine. Enveloppé de murs de briques rouges, doté d'un plafond voûté également en briques et de sol en ciment poli, cet appartement se définit par un design minimaliste saisissant. En effet, le cœur de l'espace est occupé par un module de salle de bains très original, enveloppé d'une toile métallique sculptée dont la translucidité varie en fonction de la lumière. La salle de bains et le salon couvrent la moitié de l'espace, le reste abrite la cuisine et la salle à manger. Grâce à trois unités mobiles séparées, la cuisine peut se transformer en un coin repas informel. Pour garantir l'authenticité des matériaux et accentuer leur potentiel esthétique, tous les fils électriques, prises, interrupteurs et chauffage ont été intégrés dans le sol de ciment.

Diese Wohnung befindet sich im dritten Stock eines Fabrikgebäudes aus Ziegel aus dem späten 19. Jh., und die Konstruktionselemente des Gebäudes wurden in die Gestaltung miteinbezogen. Die Wände aus rotem Ziegelstein, die gewölbte Ziegeldecke und der Boden aus poliertem Zement sind minimale Elemente mit einer überwältigenden Wirkung. Im Zentrum des Raums befindet sich eine unkonventionelle Badezimmerstruktur, gehalten von geformten Maschendraht aus Metall, der je nach einströmender Lichtmenge mehr oder weniger lichtdurchlässig ist. Das Badezimmer und der Wohnbereich nehmen die Hälfte des Raums ein, während die andere Hälfte als Küche und Essbereich dient. Mittels drei getrennter, mobiler Kücheneinheiten kann man den Kochbereich in einen zwanglosen Essbereich umgestalten. Um die originalen Konstruktionsmaterialien noch ästhetischer wirken zu lassen, befinden sich alle Elektrokabel, Steckdosen, Schalter und die Heizung im Betonboden.

An unconventional bathroom pod is contained within a sculpted wire mesh, whose translucency varies according to the light it receives.

Un module de salle de bains très original est enveloppé d'une toile métallique sculptée, dont la translucidité varie en fonction de la lumière.

Eine ungewöhnliche Badezimmerstruktur befindet sich inmitten von geformtem Maschendraht, dessen Lichtdurchlässigkeit variiert.

A free-standing basin unit includes storage facilities without occupying much space inside the bathroom pod.

Une unité de lavabo autoportante accueille des possibilités de rangement sans prendre de place à l'intérieur du module de salle de bains.

Ein freistehendes Waschbecken mit Abstellraum spart Platz in der Badezimmerstruktur.

☐ Attic in Kreuzberg
Attique à Kreuzberg
Dachgeschoss in Kreuzberg

Peanutz Architekten

This attic was built to take advantage of a gap left by an old staircase inside a telephone factory. Its high ceilings and verticality prompted the architects to convert it into a multi-level space. A surface area of 1,320 square feet was distributed over three levels. The entrance, near the kitchen, which forms part of the building's original stairwell, opens onto a twenty-three-foot-high space. The open-plan kitchen is contained within a U-shaped module of closets and drawers; beyond that, there lies a dining table with glass doors looking out on the exterior. A kitchen closet was designed to incorporate steps that lead up to the second level—a steel mezzanine structure containing a bedroom suspended from a series of steel beams. The use of steel is an attractive finish that refers to the industrial character of the original surroundings.

Cet attique a été construit pour tirer parti d'un vide laissé par la cage d'escalier d'une ancienne centrale téléphonique. Grâce à la hauteur de plafond et à la verticalité, les architectes ont optimisé l'espace pour le convertir en un loft à plusieurs niveaux. La surface de 122 m² s'articule sur trois niveaux. L'entrée, près de la cuisine, à la place du puits de l'escalier d'origine, s'ouvre sur un espace de set metres de haut. La cuisine ouverte est intégrée à un module d'armoires et de tiroirs en forme de U. Au-delà, il y a une table avec des portes en verre tournées vers l'extérieur. Le design d'un meuble de cuisine intègre des marches qui mènent au deuxième niveau —une mezzanine à ossature d'acier dotée d'un lit suspendu par une série de poutres en métal. L'emploi de l'acier donne un fini tout en élégance qui n'est pas sans rappeler l'origine industrielle du lieu.

Beim Bau dieses Lofts wurde die Lücke, die eine Treppe in dieser ehemaligenTelefonfabrik hinterlassen hat, ausgenutzt. Die hohen Decken und die Vertikalität brachten die Architekten auf die Idee, ein Loft mit mehreren Ebenen zu gestalten. 122 m² wurden auf drei Ebenen verteilt. Der Eingang in der Nähe der Küche, der zur ehemaligen Treppenhaus gehört, öffnet sich zu einem 7 Meter hohen Raum. Die offene Küche befindet sich in einem U-förmigen Modul mit Schränken und Schubladen. Ein Küchenschrank enthält die Stufen zur zweiten Ebene, ein Zwischengeschoss aus Stahl, in dem sich ein Schlafzimmer befindet, das an Stahlstangen hängt. Der industrielle Charakter dieser Wohnumgebung wird durch die Verwendung von edel wirkendem Stahl noch unterstrichen.

Another bedroom is set in a space similar to the steel mezzanine, which is reached via by the main staircase that originates on the lower floor.

Une autre chambre à coucher est installée dans un espace semblable à la mezzanine d'acier. Elle est desservie par un escalier qui part de l'étage inférieur.

Ein weiteres Schlafzimmer befindet sich in diesem Zwischengeschoss aus Stahl, das man über eine Treppe von der unteren Etage erreicht.

A network of metal beams and light rails are fixed along the brick walls to meticulously light the interior spaces.

Un réseau de poutres de métal et de rails d'éclairage est fixé le long des murs en briques, dispensant un éclairage très étudié des espaces intérieurs.

Ein Netz aus Metallstangen und Lichtschienen an der Backsteinwand beleuchtet die Räume mit Präzision.

☐ Flex House
Maison Flex
Flex Haus

Archikubik

The underlying concept for this project was to allow the residents to modify their home according to their needs while encouraging light to circulate throughout. The architect divided the space into a day zone and a night zone; these zones are separated by the element that constitutes the bathroom: a cube whose walls do not reach the ceiling and which can be integrated into the apartment on one side or the other. This solution preserves the loft's sensation of open space and allows the wooden ceiling beams to remain exposed. The various spaces are divided by panels, mobile containers, and structural pieces of furniture. A red panel can either divide the living room into two parts or separate the kitchen from the dining room. This red element integrates all the settings and contrasts with the white walls elsewhere. For the floors, the architect used a smooth concrete veneer in order to emphasize spatial continuity.

Ce projet a été conçu pour permettre aux résidents de moduler leur maison selon leurs besoins tout en laissant la lumière circuler dans tout l'appartement. L'architecte a divisé l'espace en zone de jour et zone de nuit partagées par l'élément constituant la salle de bains : un cube dont les murs ne vont pas jusqu'au plafond et dont l'intégration est possible d'un côté comme de l'autre. Cette solution permet de garder la sensation d'espace ouvert propre au loft et permet de conserver les poutres de bois apparentes. Les divers espaces sont séparés par des panneaux, des containers mobiles et des meubles qui structurent l'espace. Un panneau rouge divise le salon en deux et sépare la cuisine de la salle à manger. Cet élément rouge fait partie de l'agencement et contraste avec la blancheur des murs. L'architecte a prévu pour les sols la douceur d'un béton vernis afin d'exalter la fluidité de l'espace.

Die grundlegende Idee dieses Umbaus war es, dass die Bewohner ihr Zuhause ihren Bedürfnissen entsprechend verändern können und dass das Tageslicht in alle Winkel gelangt. So wurde der Raum in einen Bereich für den Tag und einen für die Nacht aufgeteilt. Diese Bereiche werden durch ein Element getrennt, das das Badezimmer enthält, ein Würfel, dessen Wände nicht bis zur Decke reichen und der auf beiden Seiten in die Wohnung integriert werden kann. So wirkt der Raum offen und die Dachbalken bleiben ein sichtbares, dekoratives Element. Die verschiedenen Bereiche sind durch Paneele, mobile Container und strukturelle Möbelstücke unterteilt. Mit einem roten Paneel kann das Wohnzimmer in zwei Bereiche unterteilt oder die Küche vom Esszimmer abgetrennt werden. Dieses rote Element enthält alle Einrichtungen und kontrastiert mit den übrigen weißen Wänden. Der Fußboden ist einheitlich aus glattem Betonstrich, was die Kontinuität der Räume noch unterstreicht.

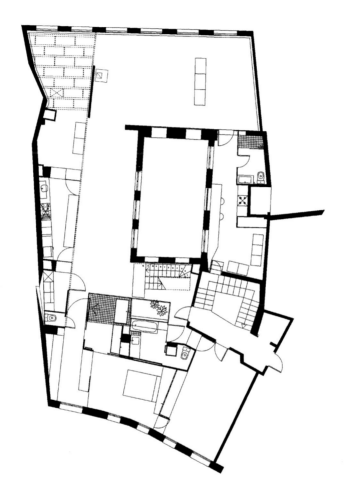

Plan Plan Grundriss

The bathroom is the element that links or separates the social area from the sleeping space.

La salle de bains est l'élément qui relie ou sépare la zone familiale de la zone de nuit.

Das Badezimmer ist das verbindende oder trennende Element zwischen Wohn- und Schlafbereich.

Flexibility was achieved by using light materials to make mobile elements.

Flexibilité issue de l'emploi de matériaux légers pour créer des éléments mobiles.

Bewegliche Elemente aus leichten Materialien sorgen für Flexibilität.

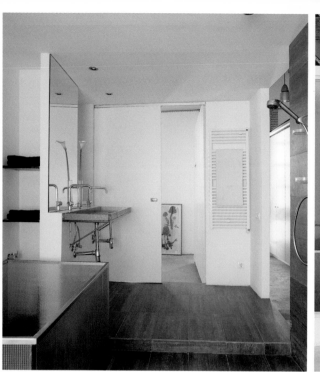

Inside the bathroom, the details, finishing, and furnishings were designed to merge with the surroundings.

Dans la salle de bains, détails, finitions et mobilier sont conçus pour fusionner avec l'environnement.

Die Möbel, Oberflächen und Dekoration des Badezimmers verschmelzen mit der Umgebung.

☐ Moerkerke House
Maison Moerkerke
Moerkerke Haus

John Pawson

In this project, a traditional Victorian mews was converted into a home for three people. In order to take better advantage of the limited space available, the kitchen, bathroom and stairs were relocated. The bottom floor, which contains the kitchen, living room, and dining room, was left as open as possible to create a large continuous space, which may be subdivided if necessary. Two further elements were added to modify the proportions of the interior space and to satisfy the home's functional needs: a chimney wall containing a staircase, and a wall that both defines and conceals the kitchen, with a stainless steel canopy above the cooker. The staircase, which is squeezed tightly against the chimney wall, is generously lit from the skylight above. Both upstairs and downstairs, the flooring is made of cherry wood, while the walls, painted white all over, create a calm atmosphere that fosters reflection.

Ce projet propose la transformation d'écuries victoriennes traditionnelles en un logement pour trois personnes. Afin d'exploiter au maximum l'espace limité disponible, la cuisine, la salle de bains et l'escalier ont été déplacés. L'ouverture du rez-de-chaussée qui abrite la cuisine, le salon et la salle à manger, a été maximalisée pour créer un grand espace fluide, susceptible d'être divisé si nécessaire. Deux autres éléments ont été ajoutés pour modifier les proportions de l'espace intérieur et satisfaire aux fonctions domestiques : un mur de cheminée contenant une cage d'escalier et un autre mur qui définit et masque la cuisine dotée d'une hotte en inox au-dessus de la cuisinière. L'escalier, coincé contre le mur de la cheminée, est parfaitement éclairé par le velux au-dessus. En haut comme en bas, le parquet est en bois de merisier et les murs entièrement peints en blanc créent une atmosphère calme qui incite à la réflexion.

Eine traditionelle, viktorianische Stallung wurde zu einem Zuhause für drei Personen umgestaltet. Um den begrenzten Raum bestmöglich auszunutzen, wurden die Küche, das Bad und die Treppe versetzt. Das Erdgeschoss, in dem sich Küche, Wohn- und Esszimmer befinden, wurde so offen wie möglich gelassen, um einen durchgehenden Raum zu schaffen, der wiederum unterteilt werden kann, falls notwendig. Zwei weitere Elemente kamen hinzu, um die Proportionen der Räume zu ändern und den Bedürfnissen der Bewohner zu entsprechen, eine Kaminwand mit einer Treppe, und eine Wand, die die Küche definiert und verbirgt und mit einer Dunstabzugshaube aus Edelstahl versehen ist. Die Treppe, die sich leicht an die Kaminwand anlehnt, erhält von einem Dachfenster reichlich Tageslicht. In beiden Stockwerken ist der Fußboden mit Kirschbaumholz belegt und die Wände sind überall weiß gestrichen, was eine ruhige, meditative Atmosphäre entstehen lässt.

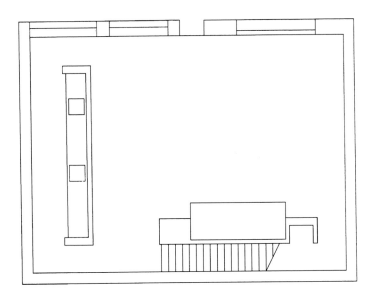

Ground floor Rez-de-chaussée Erdgeschoss

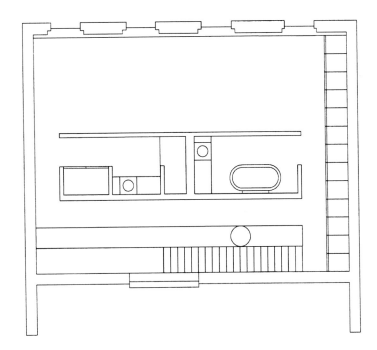

First floor Premier étage Erstes Obergeschoss

The floor is of made of cherry wood while the walls are all painted white to create a calm atmosphere that encourages reflection.

Le parquet est en bois de merisier et les murs entièrement peints en blanc créent une atmosphère calme qui incite à la réflexion.

Der mit Kirschbaum belegte Boden und die weißen Wände schaffen eine ruhige, meditative Umgebung.

The few pieces of furniture that alter the perception of the interior are the work of distinguished designers: the dining room chairs are by Wegner and the armchairs by Christian Liagre.

Les rares meubles qui influencent la perception de l'intérieur sont l'œuvre de designers renommés : les chaises du salon sont signées Wegner et les fauteuils sont l'œuvre de Christian Liagre.

Die wenigen, gezielt eingesetzten Möbel stammen von bekannten Designern, die Stühle sind von Wegner und die Sessel von Christian Liagre.

The vertical partitions are designed to appear subtle and light; they are separated from both the floor and the ceiling.

Les cloisons verticales sont conçues pour être élégantes et légères : elles ne touchent ni le sol ni le plafond.

Die vertikalen Raumteiler wirken subtil und leicht, sie berühren weder den Boden noch die Decke.

☐ Paoletti Apartment
Appartement Paoletti
Appartement Paoletti

Avatar Architettura

Set in a medieval building in the historical center, this project incorporated the transformation of a small space into an apartment for a young couple. The design explores the concept of a "habitable floor space" that is truly comfortable in its own right. The occupants can thus sit on the floor just as if it were a piece of furniture. The levelling of the cement produces variations in color that are mimicked on the walls. The materials used are left to evolve and express their own personality, exposed to inevitable weathering, thus contributing to the style characteristic of the home. The wooden floors obtained from scaffolding, rusty iron, unpolished plaster, and exposed limestone all evoke the passing of time and offer a wide range of tactile experiences on a day-to-day basis. Earthy colors predominate and plants emphasize the organic nature of the space.

Situé dans un immeuble moyenâgeux du centre historique de Florence, ce projet s'articule autour de la transformation d'un petit espace en un appartement pour un jeune couple. Le design exploite le concept de surface habitable sous l'angle d'un certain confort. Les occupants peuvent donc s'asseoir sur le sol comme si c'était un meuble. Le nivellement du ciment donne une couleur qui est reproduite sur les murs. Les matériaux employés à l'état brut doivent évoluer selon leur caractère, exposé à l'inévitable patine du temps, imprimant ainsi un certain style à la demeure. Les planchers récupérés d'échafaudages, le fer rouillé, le plâtre dépoli et le grés brut, toutes ces matières évoquent le temps qui passe et offrent un large éventail d'expériences tactiles quotidiennes. Les tons couleur terre prédominent et les plantes accentuent la nature organique de l'espace.

In diesem mittelalterliche Gebäude im historischen Stadtkern wurde eine kleine Wohnung für ein junges Paar umgebaut. Das Gestaltungskonzept ist ein bewohnbarer Fußboden, der wirklich komfortabel ist. Die Bewohner können auf dem Boden sitzen, als ob er ein Möbelstück wäre. Durch das Ebnen des Zements entstanden Farbvarianten, die an den Wänden nachgeahmt werden. Die benutzten Materialien drücken ihre eigene Persönlichkeit aus und entwickeln sich weiter, da sie dem Wetter ausgesetzt sind. So tragen sie zu dem charakteristischen Stil dieser Wohnung bei. Holzfußböden aus Gerüsten, rostiges Eisen, unpolierter Gips und sichtbarer Kalkstein erinnern an die Vergänglichkeit und ermöglichen zugleich jeden Tag neue Erfahrungen beim Ertasten. Durch Erdfarben und Pflanzen wirkt der Raum sehr organisch.

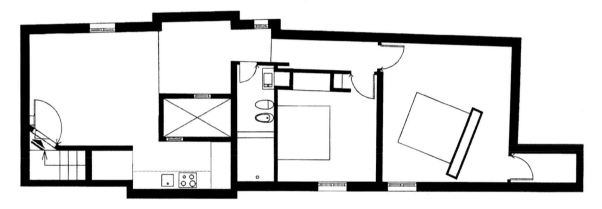

Plan Plan Grundriss

Most of the interior design, including the sofa, poof, table and pottery, was designed by Valeria Paoletti.

L'essentiel du design intérieur, y compris le divan, le pouf, la table et les poteries, porte la signature de Valeria Paoletti.

Der größte Teil der Innengestaltung einschließlich Sofa, Puff, Tisch und Keramiken wurde von Valeria Paoletti entworfen.

The design explores the concept of a "habitable floor space" that is truly comfortable in its own right.

Le design exploite le concept de « surface habitable » sous l'angle d'un certain confort.

Das Gestaltungskonzept ist ein "bewohnbarer Fußboden", der wirklich komfortabel ist.

Earth tones predominate, while plants emphasize the organic nature of the space.

Les tons couleur terre prédominent et les plantes accentuent la nature organique de l'espace.

Durch die dominierenden Erdfarben und Pflanzen wirkt der Raum sehr organisch.

☐ Apartment in Dornbirn
Appartement à Dornbirn
Appartement in Dornbirn

Geli Salzmann

The house containing this apartment was originally a tavern and blacksmith's foundry in a small, idyllic square in Dornbirn, Austria. The apartment is situated in the upper part of the structure, just below the building's sloping roof, which gives the interior space its pronounced triangular shape. The service areas, including the toilet, shower, and storage facilities, are separated by units that stop short of the ceiling. The interior design highlights the interaction between the visible parts of the building's original structure and the superbly finished surfaces and furnishings that combine wooden panels, plasterboard, stucco, and marble. The wooden furnishings consist of pieces designed to perform multiple functions.

La maison qui abrite cet appartement était à l'origine une taverne puis une forge, située sur une petite place idyllique de Dornbirn, en Autriche. L'appartement se trouve en haut du bâtiment, juste sous le pinacle, imposant à l'intérieur une forme triangulaire prononcée. Les zones de service, comprenant les toilettes, la douche et un cagibi sont séparées par des unités qui ne touchent pas le plafond. Le design intérieur souligne l'interaction entre les parties visibles d'origine, les finitions de surfaces et l'aménagement superbe mariant lambris, placoplâtre, stuc et marbre. Le mobilier en bois est constitué de pièces de design polyvalentes.

Das Haus, in dem sich diese Wohnung befindet, war einst eine Schenke und Hufschmiede an einem kleinen, idyllischen Platz in Dornbirn in Österreich. Die Wohnung befindet sich oben, genau unter dem geneigten Dach, das den Raum dreieckig macht. Küche, Bad einschließlich Toilette, Dusche und Lagerplatz sind durch Einheiten abgetrennt, die nicht bis zur Decke reichen. Bei der Raumgestaltung wurde die Beziehung zwischen den sichtbaren Teilen der Originalstruktur des Gebäudes und schön gestalteten Oberflächen und Möbeln, die Holzpaneele, gemauerte Regale, Stuck und Marmor kombinieren, unterstrichen. Die Holzmöbel sind Einzelstücke, die mehreren Funktionen gleichzeitig dienen können.

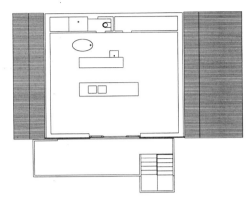

Plan Plan Grundriss

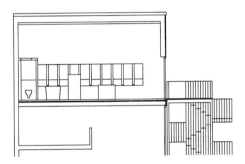

Longitudinal section Section longitudinale Längsschnitt

Cross section Section transversale Querschnitt

The distinctive appearance of this setting is achieved by combining contemporary pieces with more rustic objects and materials.

Cet agencement tient son originalité de l'alliance entre des meubles contemporains et les objets et matériaux plus rustiques.

Durch die Kombination zeitgenössischer Elemente mit rustikalen Objekten und Materialien entstand eine außergewöhnliche Atmosphäre.

With a touch of playful whimsy, the Austrian artist Edith Grabher has placed golden antlers on a surface painted to look like the sky.
Clin d'œil sympathique : l'artiste autrichienne Edith Grabher a placé des bois de cerf en or sur une surface peinte comme un ciel.
Die österreichische Künstlerin Edith Grabher hat als kleine Spielerei ein goldenes Geweih auf einen gemalten Himmel gesetzt.

e wooden furnishings consist of pieces designed to perform multiple functions. The kitchen worktop is also the dining table and the sideboard forms the rear part of the bathroom.

ameublement en bois est fait d'éléments conçus pour être polyvalents. Le plan de travail de la cuisine sert aussi de table et le buffet forme l'arrière de la salle de bains.

e Holzmöbel sind Einzelstücke mit mehreren Funktionen. Die Arbeitsfläche der Küche ist gleichzeitig Esstisch und das Regal formt die Badezimmerwand.

The space is organized around two pieces laid out parallel to the entrance: the large table that serves as the dining area, and the sideboard that marks off the bathroom.

L'espace s'articule autour de deux éléments installés parallèlement à l'entrée : la grande table qui sert de zone de salle à manger et le buffet qui délimite la salle de bains.

Der Raum wird durch zwei parallel laufende Elemente aufgeteilt, den großen Esstisch und das Regal, das das Bad abtrennt.

Residence in Munich
Résidence à Munich
Wohnung in München

Siggi Pfundt/Form Werkstatt

Located in the center of Munich, this apartment forms part of what was previously a sewing-machine factory in the city's old industrial area. In order to divide up the apartment, the architect installed five modular chipboard panels hanging from a metal rail. These elements accentuate the longitudinal axis of the unit and separate the private and social areas. As a result, the bedroom – differentiated from the rest of the home by its wooden floor – can remain isolated from the living room and work area, or it can become part of the large open space. The social and work areas are grouped along the façade in order to make the most of the space's only source of light. The cement floor alludes to the industrial spirit of the old factory and blends with the wood and metal to create warmth in this factory-turned-apartment.

Situé au centre de Munich, cet appartement fait partie de ce qui était auparavant une usine de machines à coudre dans l'ancien quartier industriel de la cité. Pour diviser l'appartement, l'architecte a installé cinq panneaux modulaires en contreplaqué suspendu à un rail de métal. Ils permettent d'accentuer l'axe longitudinal de l'unité et de séparer les sphères privées et publiques. Par conséquent, la chambre à coucher – qui diffère du reste des pièces par son parquet – peut être isolée du salon et du bureau ou peut intégrer le grand espace ouvert. Les aires d'accueil et de travail sont regroupées le long de la façade pour tirer parti de l'unique source de lumière de l'espace. Les sols en ciment rappèlent le caractère industriel de l'ancien bâtiment et se conjuguent harmonieusement avec le bois et le métal pour créer une ambiance chaleureuse dans cette usine transformée en appartement.

Dieses Appartement im Zentrum von München liegt in einer alten Nähmaschinenfabrik im ehemaligen Industriegebiet der Stadt. Um die Wohnung zu unterteilen, installierte der Architekt fünf modulare Paneele aus Spanplatten, die an einer Metallschiene hängen. Diese Elemente betonen die Längsachse der Einheit und trennen die privaten von den allgemein genutzten Bereichen ab. Deshalb kann das Schlafzimmer, das im Gegensatz zur restlichen Wohnung einen Holzfußboden hat, vom Wohn- und Arbeitsbereich abgetrennt werden, oder es kann Teil eines großen, offenen Raumes werden. Die Wohn- und Arbeitsbereiche liegen an der Fassade, um die einzige Lichtquelle so gut wie möglich zu nutzen. Der Zementboden erinnert an die industrielle Vergangenheit des Gebäudes und in Kombination mit dem Holz und Metall lässt er diese Fabrikwohnung sehr warm wirken.

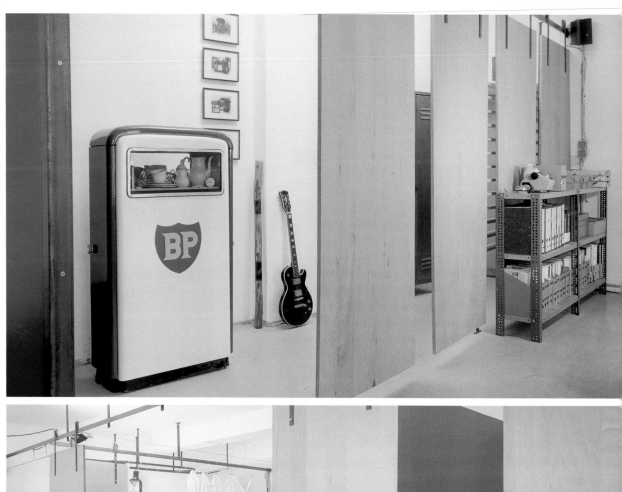

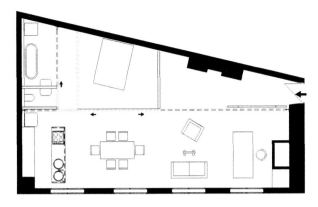

Plan Plan Grundriss

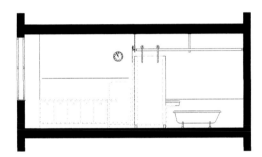

Cross section Section transversale Querschnitt

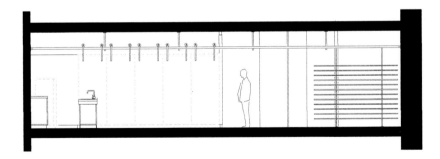

Longitudinal section Section longitudinale Längsschnitt

The architect opted for birch plywood so that the panels could be maneuvered with ease and the renovation endowed with warmth.

L'architecte a choisi le contreplaqué de bouleau pour manœuvrer les cloisons facilement et pour réaliser une restauration chaleureuse.

Der Architekt schuf Paneele aus Sperrholz mit Birkenfurnier, die leicht zu bewegen sind und sehr warm wirken.

Apartment in Janelas Verdes
Appartement à Janelas Verdes
Appartement in Janelas Verdes

João Maria Ventura

The aim of this project was to turn this two-story space into a comfortable home for a single person. On the upper level, which contains the entrance, space was freed up as much as possible to create a long, narrow living room. At one end, an opening on to the courtyard offers a view of the tree that grows there. The bathroom and kitchen are located on one side of this level, with a small dining niche near the window. The lower floor contains the bedroom, defined by four walls, the laundry room, placed under the stairs, and the exit on to the courtyard. The impact of the limited floor space and low height is minimized by the light that filters through the leaves of the tree. Painting all the walls white made the best of these far-from-perfect conditions.

Le but de ce projet était de transformer cet espace à deux étages en un logement confortable pour une seule personne. Au niveau supérieur où se trouve l'entrée, l'espace a été libéré au maximum pour créer un long salon étroit, avec une ouverture à l'une de ses extrémités qui donne sur un atrium et sur l'arbre qui y pousse. La salle de bains et la cuisine sont situées d'un côté de ce niveau avec un petit coin repas, niché près de la fenêtre. L'étage inférieur abrite la chambre à coucher définie par quatre murs, la buanderie, située sous l'escalier et l'accès à l'atrium. L'impact de cet espace réduit et de la faible hauteur de plafond est atténué par l'action de la lumière filtrée à travers les feuilles de l'arbre. Les murs ont été peints en blanc : optimisation astucieuse de ces conditions de base peu favorables.

Ein zweistöckiger Raum sollte in ein komfortables Zuhause für eine Person umgebaut werden. Auf der oberen Ebene befindet sich der Eingang. Der Raum wurde so weit wie möglich geleert, um ein langes und enges Wohnzimmer zu schaffen. An einem Ende blickt man durch eine Öffnung zum Hof und sieht den Baum, der dort wächst. Das Bad und die Küche befinden sich auf einer Seite dieser Ebene. Es gibt einen kleinen Essbereich in Fensternähe. Auf der unteren Etage befinden sich das von vier Wänden definierte Schlafzimmer, das Wäschezimmer unter der Treppe und der Ausgang zum Hof. Das Licht, das durch die Blätter des Baums gefiltert wird, mildert den Eindruck, den der beschränkte Platz und die niedrige Höhe hinterlassen. Um das Beste aus dieser wirklich schwierigen Umgebung zu machen, wurden alle Wände weiß gestrichen.

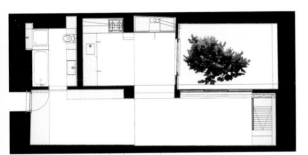

First floor Premier étage Erstes Obergeschoss

Ground floor Rez-de-chaussée Erdgeschoss

Longitudinal section Section longitudinale Längsschnitt

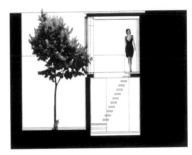

Cross section Section transversale Querschnitt

An interior courtyard provides the apartment with the natural light and ventilation necessary for a home.

Une cour intérieure procure la lumière naturelle et la ventilation nécessaires à l'appartement.

Durch einen Innenhof fällt Tageslicht in die Wohnung und es wird für Belüftung gesorgt.

Painting all the walls white made the most of these far from ideal conditions.

Peindre les murs en blanc est la meilleure façon de tirer parti de ces conditions loin d'être idéales.

Um das Beste aus dieser wirklich schwierigen Umgebung zu machen, wurden alle Wände weiß gestrichen.

☐ Bollarino Apartment
Appartement Bollarino
Appartement Bollarino

W. Camagna, M. Camoletto, A. Marcante/UdA

This apartment was created as a result of the restoration of an old home in the heart of Turin, Italy. The main challenge was to link the glass-enclosed balcony, with its view of the garden, to the rest of the existing space. To accomplish this, the dividers that previously broke up the space were almost entirely eliminated. Only the structural walls were retained, and these served as a point of departure for marking off the various areas. The three original rooms were replaced by a generous, continuous space. The bathroom with a shower takes on a great formal richness that blends with the existing wall, the glass skylight, the painted metal beams, and the glass sliding doors. The permeability of the space and the play of reflections produced by the glass are also visible from the outside.

Cet appartement est le fruit de la restauration d'une ancienne maison située au cœur de Turin, en Italie. Le plus grand défi à relever était de réunir le balcon entouré de vitrages, donnant sur le jardin, au reste de l'espace existant. Pour y parvenir, les cloisons divisant l'espace antérieur ont été presque entièrement supprimées. Seuls les murs de structure ont été maintenus comme point de départ à la restructuration de l'espace en diverses zones. Les trois pièces antérieures forment désormais un vaste espace continu. La salle de bains dotée d'une douche gagne une grande richesse formelle en harmonie avec les murs existants, le velux, les colonnes peintes en couleur métallique et les portes de verre coulissantes. La transparence de l'espace et les jeux de lumières issus du verre sont également visibles de l'extérieur.

Dieses Appartement wurde geschaffen, als man ein altes Haus im Zentrum von Turin in Italien renovierte. Wichtigstes Ziel der Gestalter war es, den verglasten Balkon mit Blick auf den Garten in den übrigen Raum zu integrieren. Dazu wurden zunächst fast alle Trennwände entfernt. Nur die tragende Wand blieb erhalten und diente als Ausgangspunkt für die Raumaufteilung. Die drei ursprünglichen Zimmer wurden zu einem durchgehenden, weiten Raum. Das Badezimmer mit der Dusche ist mit interessanten Elementen wie der bereits existierenden Wand, dem Dachfenster, den gestrichenen Metallträgern und der gläsernen Schiebetür sehr reich gestaltet. Die Durchlässigkeit des Raums und das Spiel der Reflexe, das durch das Glas entsteht, sind auch von außen sichtbar.

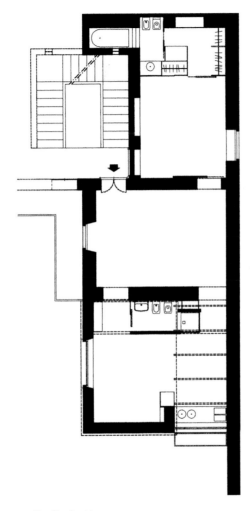

Plan Plan Grundriss

Opening up the interior space made it possible to enjoy views of the garden from almost anywhere in the apartment.

L'ouverture de l'espace intérieur permet de jouir de la vue sur le jardin de n'importe quel endroit de l'appartement, ou presque.

Durch Öffnen des Innenraums sieht man von fast überall in der Wohnung in den Garten.

Red metal beams create a dynamism that interacts with the structural walls.

Des poutres en métal rouge diffusent un dynamisme en interaction avec les murs structuraux.

Rote Metallstangen lassen eine Dynamik entstehen, die mit den tragenden Wänden im Wechselspiel steht.

The details and finishing are striking in their simplicity. A set of three sliding doors in the bedroom makes the entrance to the bathroom and closet a subtle composition.

Les détails et l'agencement frappent par leur sobriété. Dans la chambre à coucher, un ensemble élégant de trois portes coulissantes marque l'entrée vers la salle de bains et le dressing.

Die Details und Materialien sind sehr einfach. Drei Schiebetüren im Schlafzimmer bilden den Eingang zum Bad und zur Toilette, ein subtile Komposition.

Apartment on Flinders Lane
Appartement sur la Flinders Lane
Appartement in Flinders Lane

Tom McCallum, Shania Shegedyn

This space is located in an old office building in the heart of Melbourne, Australia, that was converted into an apartment complex. The project is defined by two main elements. The first is a multifunctional, free-standing wood-framed unit that encloses the sleeping area, provides storage space, serves as an auxiliary dining room, includes bookshelves, and is a sculptural element in its own right. This unit, looking almost like a piece of furniture, is free-standing and touches neither the ceiling nor the side walls. The second element is the set of patterns sandblasted into the original cement floor. These patterns, with their polished texture, are reminiscent of the diagrams used by the architects in their design plans and contrast with the previous floor covering. The space was left completely open and the patterns on the floor simply suggest ways to approach the layout and accommodate the furnishings.

Cet espace est situé dans d'anciens bureaux, au cœur de Melbourne, en Australie, convertis en un complexe de logements. Deux critères essentiels définissent ce projet. Le premier est un module à châssis en bois, polyvalent et autoportant. Il comprend la partie chambres, procure de l'espace de rangement, sert de salle à manger auxiliaire, possède des étagères intégrées et est un élément sculptural à part entière. Cette unité, à l'instar d'un meuble, est autoportante et ne touche ni le plafond, ni les murs latéraux. Le deuxième élément est un ensemble de motifs projetés au sable dans le sol en ciment d'origine. Ces motifs, à la texture vernie, sont une réminiscence des diagrammes utilisés par les architectes dans leur plan de conception et contrastent avec le revêtement préalable du sol. L'espace est complètement ouvert et les motifs sur les sols suggèrent tout simplement des façons de comprendre le plan et d'aménager l'intérieur.

Diese Wohnung befindet sich in einem alten Bürohaus mitten in Melbourne, Australien, das zu einem Appartementkomplex umgebaut wurde. Zwei wichtige Elemente prägen den Raum. Einmal die multifunktionelle, freistehende und mit Holz umrahmte Einheit, in der sich der Schlafbereich und Lagerraum befinden, und die als behelfsmäßiges Esszimmer benutzt werden kann. In dieser Einheit, die in sich selbst bereits ein skulpturelles Element ist, gibt es Bücherregale. Die Einheit, die fast wie ein Möbelstück aussieht, steht frei und berührt weder die Decke noch die Seitenwände. Das zweite Element sind die sandgestrahlten Muster auf dem alten Zementboden. Diese Muster mit ihrer glatten Textur erinnern an die Diagramme, die Architekten in ihren Plänen benutzen und sie bilden einen Kontrast zu dem vorherigen Bodenbelag. Der Raum wurde völlig offen gelassen und die Muster auf dem Boden schlagen einfach nur Möglichkeiten für die Verteilung der Funktionen und Anordnung der Möbel vor.

Plan Plan Grundriss

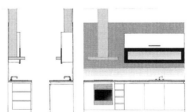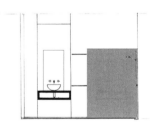

Elevations Élévations Aufrisse

A multifunctional, free-standing wood-framed unit encloses the sleeping area, as well as providing storage space and bookshelves.

Un module à châssis en bois, polyvalent et autoportant comprend la partie chambres, avec en plus de l'espace de rangement et des étagères.

Eine multifunktionelle, freistehende und mit Holz umrahmte Einheit umgibt den Schlafbereich und enthält einen Lagerraum und Bücherregale.

This unit is free-standing, touches neither the ceiling nor the side walls, and looks almost like a piece of furniture.

Cette unité est autoportante : elle ne touche ni le plafond ni les murs latéraux et à des allures de meuble.

Diese Einheit, die fast wie ein Möbelstück aussieht, steht frei und berührt weder die Decke noch die Seitenwände.

West Village Apartment
Appartement à West Village
Appartement in West Village

Desai/Chia Studio

The design of this apartment had to be flexible enough to permit entertaining and accommodate visitors for short periods in a minimal space. After removing the partitions that divided the interior, the designers concentrated all the activities in a central space. Grouping the service areas, such as the kitchen, bathroom, and laundry room, on a side wall ensured efficient use of the space while optimizing the placement of fixtures. A small attic bedroom above the kitchen was built with thin strips of stainless steel to leave as much space as possible both above and below the platform. In addition to creating a small extra bedroom, it acts as a backdrop for the living area. A storage unit made of lacquered panels is the only element separating the bedroom from the rest of the apartment. Lights built into the loft's structure illuminate the kitchen as well as the sleeping area, while the wooden planks add a touch of warmth to both spots.

Le design de cet appartement devait être assez flexible pour loger des visiteurs sur des courtes périodes dans un minimum d'espace. Après avoir décloisonné l'intérieur, les designers ont réuni toutes les activités dans un espace central. Le regroupement des zones de service, à l'instar de la cuisine, de la salle de bains et de la buanderie sur un mur latéral a permis une exploitation efficace de l'espace en optimisant l'emplacement des équipements et accessoires. Une petite chambre sous les combles, au-dessus de la cuisine a été construite en minces bandes d'acier inoxydable, pour un maximum d'espace libre en dessous et au-dessus de la plate-forme. Cette petite chambre annexe ainsi créée, offre une toile de fond au salon. Une unité de rangement en panneaux laqués est l'unique cloison qui sépare la chambre du reste de l'appartement. Un éclairage intégré au plafond illumine à la fois la cuisine et la partie chambre. Les poutres en bois ajoutent une touche chaleureuse aux deux espaces.

Die Gestaltung dieses Appartements musste flexibel genug sein, um Besucher für kürzere Zeit auf kleinem Raum unterbringen zu können. Nachdem alle Raumteiler entfernt waren, konzentrierten die Gestalter alle Aktivitäten in einem zentralen Raum. Funktionelle Bereiche wie Küche, Badezimmer und Wäscheraum liegen auf einer Seite, so dass der Platz effizient für alle Installationen genutzt wurde. Ein kleines Schlafzimmer unter dem Dach über der Küche wurde mit dünnen Edelstahlstreifen gebaut, so dass über und unter der Plattform soviel Platz wie möglich blieb. Zusätzlich wurde ein kleines, zusätzliches Schlafzimmer geschaffen, das den Hintergrund des Wohnbereiches bildet. Eine Lagereinheit aus lackierten Paneelen ist das einzige Element, das das Schlafzimmer vom Rest der Wohnung abtrennt. Die in die Struktur integrierten Lampen beleuchten sowohl die Küche als auch das Schlafzimmer. Holzbretter lassen beide Räume warm wirken.